MARY ELLEN MARK

Photographs of Mother Teresa's Missions of Charity in Calcutta, India

In memory of Jennifer Kapoor

M.E.M.

ISSN 0163-7916; ISBN 0-933286-43-0
Library of Congress Catalogue No. 85-80202
All rights reserved in all countries. No part
of this book may be reproduced or translated in any form
without written permission from The Friends of Photography.

UNTITLED 39.
This is the thirty-ninth in a series of publications
on serious photography by The Friends of Photography.
Some previous issues are still available.
For a list of these write to Post Office Box 500,
Carmel, California 93921.

Design by Desne Border.
Photocomposition in Bembo
by Mackenzie-Harris Corporation.
Printed with laser Fultones®
by Gardner/Fulmer Lithograph.

Acknowledgements

THE STAFF OF THE FRIENDS OF PHOTOGRAPHY first became aware of the large body of photographs Mary Ellen Mark had made of Mother Teresa's activities in Calcutta in the spring of 1983, when Mark showed them during our workshop on documentary photography. The tremendous power of the photographs was obvious, as one hundred people sat in near-total silence during the entire slide presentation.

At the time, Mark had offered the book to a number of publishers, but none had seen the work as "commercial" enough for a publication to be possible economically. Feeling that photographs of such intensity should not be denied a broad audience, David Featherstone, executive associate of The Friends, took a special interest in the project and proposed that the work be included in The Friends' publishing and exhibition programs. The exhibition he organized of Mark's Calcutta photographs opened at The Friends Gallery in Carmel in December 1983 and drew a substantial audience. Ansel Adams was also instrumental in supporting publication of this book. Particularly moved by what he had seen in the exhibition, he immediately suggested to me that we publish it as a part of the *Untitled* series.

While the subject matter of these images cannot help but take a dominant role in any publication, and while the sequence of the prints is designed to reveal the activities of the Missions of Charity, this book is also intended to highlight the remarkable abilities of the artist. The greatest thanks must go to Mary Ellen Mark for creating these photographs and for her support and cooperation throughout the project. Thanks must also go to David Featherstone for his critical introduction and for his thoughtful sequencing of the photographs. Grateful acknowledgement must be given to all of those who helped to create this important publication—Julia Nelson-Gal and John Breeden for their editorial assistance, Tory Read for her help in researching the text, Libby McCoy for her technical assistance and Gary Schneider for making the prints used in reproduction. Special thanks must go to Desne Border for her design of the book, and to David Gardner, of Gardner/Fulmer Lithograph, for assuring the quality of the reproductions.

In addition, Mary Ellen Mark conveys her gratitude to John Loengard and Melvin Scott of *Life* magazine for providing her with the initial assignment to go to Calcutta, to Ruth Prawer Jhabvala and to her husband, Martin Bell. She also wishes to thank the people of the Missions of Charity for their support.

JAMES ALINDER, *Editor*
The *Untitled* series

MOTHER TERESA, SHISHU BHAWAN, CALCUTTA, 1980

Introduction

BY DAVID FEATHERSTONE

SOCIALLY CONSCIOUS IMAGES have formed one of the dominant themes of photography throughout the twentieth century, yet documentary photographs have not normally been well received by art museums and other art-oriented institutions until the passage of time has provided an historical and aesthetic context for their presentation. In recent years, however, the hard line between art and documentation has softened. Young photographers and others who form the growing audience for serious photography, bolstered by an expanded awareness of the history and traditions of the medium, have been able to see the work of those covering the wars in Southeast Asia and Central America, for example, or of those documenting the plight of the sick, starving and homeless in India and Africa, in an expanded context.

Unlike earlier years, when the images that could serve as models for a beginning documentary photographer were only published newspaper or magazine photographs, pictures by individuals such as Jacob Riis, Lewis Hine, Dorothea Lange, W. Eugene Smith, Robert Capa and others are now frequent subjects for museum exhibitions and college courses on photographic history. The work of these individuals has come to be seen in aesthetic, as well as socio-political terms; and, by extension, the professional traditions of photojournalism are not the only qualities that inform socially conscious photography. Contemporary documentary photography has thus come to be valued not only for the information it conveys about its subject and the problems of the modern world, but also for what it reveals about the photographic medium and for the aesthetic experience it brings to its viewers.

Mary Ellen Mark is one of the photographers whose work has received this multi-faceted recognition, and the photographs presented here of Mother Teresa's Missions of Charity in Calcutta typify her concerns. Mark has always had an interest in people, and the opportunity to document a specific group within a thematic context has clearly been a motivating factor in her work. The photographs also demonstrate her unwillingness to allow an initial magazine assignment to be an end in itself. As she has often done during twenty years of photographing for publications, Mark returned to Calcutta after her commissioned project was completed in order to undertake a more intense and personal exploration of her subject.

Mark began to photograph in 1963, during her early work as a graduate student at the University of Pennsylvania's Annenberg School of Communications in Philadelphia. She had just completed an undergraduate degree in painting and art history at the university, and found her new work with photography instructor Lou Glessman, an art director for *Holiday* magazine, to be stimulating. It was a creative learning environment, with project-oriented classes that encouraged students to develop their visual sensibilities.

Remaining in Philadelphia after receiving her master's degree in 1964, Mark did her first freelance work using the school's darkroom facilities. In 1965 she received a Fulbright Fellowship, an award not normally given to visual artists, to travel and photograph in Turkey. The next year she moved to New York City, where she began to freelance for magazines. The Catholic magazine *Jubilee* and the University of Pennsylvania alumni publication provided a number of her early assignments. Mark received her first big break in magazine work through Pat Carbine, an editor for *Look* now on the editorial staff of *MS*, who gave her two assignments in Europe. The first of these, a study of Italian film director Federico Fellini, was published in *Look* in 1968; a story on London's innovative methadone program for heroin addicts followed in 1969. The subject matter of the latter essay contained elements that would consume much of her efforts in the future—health care and the plight of those cast out by society.

Mark's photographic career assumed an additional aspect in 1968, when she secured a job making production stills for the United Artists film *Alice's Restaurant*. This work on Hollywood film sets continued at intervals, providing a welcome break from the intense and heartrending situations she often photographed in the outside world. It also gave her entrance into situations that provided possibilities for personal projects. In 1974, for example, while doing stills on location for the film *One Flew over the Cuckoo's Nest*, she visited the locked ward for women at the Oregon State Mental Hospital. Struck by what she saw there, Mark made arrangements to return to Oregon after filming was completed; she spent two months photographing on the ward during 1976. The result was the book *Ward 81*, published in 1979, a sensitive and revealing look at the life of a group of women confined to a state-run hospital environment.

Mary Ellen Mark made her first trip to India in 1968. Already well-traveled, she was intrigued by the beauty and diversity of the country and has returned there some thirteen times in the succeeding years. These trips have sometimes been made on assignment for news magazines, but they have also been undertaken to complete self-assigned photographic projects. In 1978 Mark went to Bombay, where she photographed the prostitutes in the city's well-known red-light district. Some of the photographs were first published in Germany's *Stern* magazine; her book-length study *Falkland Road* was released in 1981.

Mark's second major photographic study in India began in late 1979, when she was sent by *Life* magazine to photograph the Missions of Charity in Calcutta. Mother Teresa, the order's founder and leader, had just been awarded the Nobel Peace Prize, and the photographs were to accompany a feature article on the woman. While the photographs published in *Life* successfully portrayed both the poverty of the patients and the needed service provided by the clinics, the experience in Calcutta only whetted Mark's visual appetite for a more complete study. She felt a need to go back to complete the photographic document she knew remained unresolved. By July she had made the necessary arrangements, and in January 1981 she returned to Calcutta for a two-month stay. Photographs from both of these intensive periods of work are the subject of this book.

In the years since the completion of the project on Mother Teresa, Mark has explored a variety of subjects and has actively lectured and led workshops throughout the country. Photographic projects have taken her, among other places, to Miami Beach, where she documented the lifestyle of senior citizens, to a summer camp for children terminally ill with cancer, to Zimbabwe, where she photographed the white minority that once ruled the country, and to famine-stricken Ethiopia.

An additional project that assumed great personal importance was her document of runaway children in Seattle. Done first on assignment from *Life* and published in July 1983 as "Streets of the Lost," Mark again felt that the initial work had not fully explored the subject. She spent more than two months of the following year in Seattle with her husband, filmmaker Martin Bell, and producer Cheryl McCall, providing production assistance on a film about these children cast aside by their families and often ignored by social service agencies. The rapport she had achieved with the young people in her earlier work facilitated the filming. *Streetwise*, released in 1984, was nominated for an Oscar for Best Documentary Film of the year. During the filming in Seattle, Mark was able to continue her series of still photographs for use in a future book-length publication.

Beginning in 1976, Mark was associated with Magnum, the New York and Paris-based picture agency, and many of her magazine and commercial assignments of the late 1970s came through this organization. Five years later, she joined with a group of other photographers to found Archive Pictures. Mary Ellen Mark's photographs have appeared in most photography magazines, including *American Photographer, Camera, Camera Arts, French Photo, Infinity, Leica Magazine, Modern Photography* and *Popular Photography*. The broader impact of her work can be seen in the variety of the many international publications that have printed her photographs: *Connoisseur, Esquire, Life,* the *London Sunday Times, Look, MS,* the *New York Times Magazine, Paris Match, Rolling Stone, Stern, Time, Vanity Fair* and others.

Mark has continually shown a concern for aesthetic, as well as communicative values in her photography, and one indication of the success she has achieved is that her widespread recognition has come from the fields of both art and journalism. She received fellowships from the National Endowment for the Arts in 1977 and 1979, and was awarded a New York State Council for the Arts grant in 1977. Her photographs have been included in numerous group exhibitions and have been presented in one person shows in museums and galleries throughout the country. Awards for her magazine projects are many; among the most prestigious are a first prize from the University of Missouri Pictures of the Year Awards for the photo-essay "Streets of the Lost" and first prizes from the Robert F. Kennedy Journalism Awards for her *Life* magazine stories on the summer camp for children with cancer and, before that, on Mother Teresa.

On the visit to Calcutta on which the photographs for the *Life* article were made, Mark's access to Mother Teresa had been limited. She also found it both painful and inspiring to photograph within the clinics, which were suffused in the sacred context of the Mission's unrelenting service to the poor. This intense spiritualism, combined with the impact of disease and poverty, made Mark's initial experience in Calcutta, particularly that in Nirmal Hriday, the Home for the Dying, emotionally troubling. As she usually does when photographing on a project such as this, Mark kept a journal in which she recorded not only caption material, but also her responses to what she was seeing. Excerpts from the Calcutta journals are printed with some of the images reproduced here.

On her second trip to Calcutta in 1981, at the suggestion of Sister Luke, the chief administrator of the Home for the Dying who had held the position for twenty years, Mark spent some time working in the clinics before she brought out her camera. In part a contribution exchanged for the privilege of photographing there, the experience helped her to come to terms with her earlier discomfort at photographing in such intensely moving surroundings. It also gave her time to become familiar with the patients' daily activities and more involved with them as human beings. In addition, by establishing herself more firmly within the Mission community, she was granted greater access to Mother Teresa, who traditionally spent much of her time in prayerful, self-imposed isolation.

Mark was able to photograph Mother Teresa in religious services, giving communion to the sisters of her order and as she moved through the hospital distributing food, medication and encouragement to the patients. After the helpful intervention of a Jesuit priest at the Mission, who delivered a sermon on the importance of photography, she was even granted permission to acccompany Mother Teresa on a trip to branches of the Missions of Charity in other Indian cities. While these pictures with Mother Teresa as the primary subject hold much interest, particularly for those who have come to revere her as a saintly figure, the photographs made within the clinics, of the care administered to the ill and of the relationships between the nurses and patients, and between the patients themselves, depict more pointedly the importance of Mother Teresa's work.

Mark spent most of her time photographing in the Home for the Dying, but she also visited other centers run by the Missions of Charity in and around Calcutta. These included the Nirmala Kennedy Center, a home for retarded and homeless women; Shanti Nagar (Peace) Village, a leprosy hospital four hours by train outside of the city; Shishu Bhawan, a home, adoption center and hospital for abandoned and malnourished children; and Prem Dan (Gift of Love), a large complex with facilities for caring for recovering tuberculosis patients, homeless women and retarded young boys.

One question that often arises in discussions of documentary photographs, particularly those that attempt to describe the human condition, concerns the veracity of the images, the degree to which they objectively depict what was actually there. On an obvious level, Mary Ellen Mark's photographs from Calcutta do not: they are small, two-dimensional, in monochrome rather than color; they present only an instant out of a continuum of activity. On another level they reveal a great deal about the experience of a life of malnutrition and disease; about the nature of a health care system, primitive by Western standards, that struggles valiantly to keep up with the sheer numbers of those for whom it is dedicated to caring.

Skeptics afraid to respond personally to a powerful documentary image often want to be sure that the photograph was not staged. Mary Ellen Mark assures us that her photographs were not, that they depict events frequently seen during her stay in Calcutta. It is through her inherent skill as a photographer that she anticipates visual relationships and prepares to record them by moving to the appropriate place to make the most effective photograph. Through her perceptive selection of subjects that encapsulate a range of activities or a complexity of emotions, Mark moves the viewer to feel something of what she has seen. By photographing a nurse, for example, just as she placed her hands on two patients' heads in a natural gesture of comfort (page 17), Mark heightens the archetypal associations of the image. By isolating an old woman's wrinkled arms, raised over her face in front of a shadowy room (page 41), she directly addresses the woman's condition. Similarly, in photographing a young Iranian volunteer looking directly at the camera with an expression that reveals his own shock at what he has seen in the clinics (page 39), she challenges the viewer to compare his clear and healthy face to that of the emaciated Indian for whom he is caring.

Despite this determination to make a photograph from its most effective point of view, and at the most appropriate time, few of Mark's images have the tightly structured composition that is frequently associated with images motivated by a search for the "decisive moment." Her subject matter is too intense to be treated as sterile structural elements. The photograph of a clinic waiting room (page 15), for instance, which shows a man holding a child on one side of a doorway, an older man pressed into the corner of the frame on the other side of the room and a shadowy figure approaching the door from the distance, is unusual in its classically balanced composition. Yet despite its structure, it is the people in the picture, rather than their arrangement within it, who are the subject of the photograph. While Mark frames her subjects formally, she more typically allows the importance of the activities and individuals depicted to take precedence.

This conscious intent in the photographs extends to her choice of using black and white, rather than color film for her Calcutta project. Mark is equally proficient in both media; the ability to photograph in color is a requirement for those providing visual material for modern magazines and, increasingly, newspapers. On at least one occasion Mark has photographed a story for a magazine in color, while feeling strongly that the message could be more effectively transmitted if the publisher would agree to a black and white treatment. For her personal projects she is free to select the mode that will best express the subject.

The *Falkland Road* essay, done the year before her first Calcutta visit, was photographed in color, as it only could have been. The saturated purples, reds and golds of the clothing worn by the prostitutes and their madams, the richly colored wall decorations and the warm-toned light in the rooms and on the street all enhance the sensually encompassing feeling inherent in the subject. In Mother Teresa's clinics, the colors, even if less intense, would have significantly distracted from the impact Mark wanted in the photographs. The perceptual abstraction created by the transformation of colored subjects to black and white reinforces the severity of the conditions in the Home for the Dying and eliminates the viewer's natural visual interest in the colors themselves. By stripping away the comforting surroundings of color, Mark increases the poignancy of the photographs and in a strange way allows the viewer to see them as more pointedly documentary.

By the time of Mary Ellen Mark's first visit to Calcutta, Mother Teresa's Missions of Charity had spread to some 160 institutions worldwide, half of them within India and the rest spread through 32 countries on six continents. The missionary's work was known by many prior to the awarding of the Nobel Peace Prize, and she had established an international following in both the religious and lay communities. Despite this visibility, and even though the worldwide support for Mother Teresa's projects speaks to the public compassion on which she has consistently been able to draw, the origins of her Missions were humble.

Born Agnes Bonxha Bojaxhiu to Albanian parents, in Skoplje, Yugoslavia, in 1910, Mother Teresa knew by the age of twelve that she wanted to be a missionary. She learned of work being done in India, and when she was 18 she joined a group of Loreto nuns working in Calcutta. She took her final vows in 1937 and taught in a high school for girls from the city's privileged classes; she later became its principal. In 1946 she received a call to serve "the poorest of the poor," took an intensive training course in nursing, opened a school in Moti Jheel, Calcutta's poorest slum, and formed the Missions of Charity.

A Calcutta hospital gave her a vacant hostel for use as a clinic for those found dying on the streets—a group that included, as it still does today, far too great a percentage of the city's population—and this institution became the centerpoint of her Mission. Ironically, the hostel had been used as a rest house by pilgrims visiting the adjoining Temple of Kali, a shrine to the Hindu goddess of death, destruction and purification. This association, firmly planted in the Indian public mind, helped bring about acceptance of her work; but even with this support, there were still cultural differences to be overcome in establishing the Missions. The Hindu concept of karma, for example, suggests that suffering is one way in which improper conduct during a current or earlier incarnation may be worked through; it is thus, to some extent, seen as deserved. This religious force, with its pervasive impact on Indian culture, was in direct opposition to Mother Teresa's Christian doctrine, which mandated giving aid to those who suffered. As one writer close to Mother Teresa described it in *America* magazine, "Above the head of the wasted person on a pallet in the Hostel for the Dying occurs a collision of values, of karma and reincarnation versus innocent suffering and the incarnation."

The Roman Catholic church, of course, did have active and well-established missions in India, and this conflict of cultures did little to forestall the activities of Mother Teresa and her Sisters, many of whom were Indians themselves. She became fluent in both Bengali and Hindi, and adopted as the uniform of the order the simple cotton sari of poor Indian women. Mother Teresa became a citizen of the country in 1948, and the Missions of Charity began its expansion.

Despite the nearly universal and enthusiastic approval of Mother Teresa's designation as recipient of the 1979 Nobel Prize for Peace, there was some opposition. Some groups inside India, a country historically torn by conflicting religious and political factions, were wary of what they saw as a growing Mother Teresa-ism. In the West, activist critics objected that Mother Teresa's programs did nothing to attack the structures that cause poverty; others took a strict view of the meaning of the peace award and suggested that Mother Teresa had not helped the cause of world peace, but had merely assisted the distressed. Characteristically, Mother Teresa took little notice of this opposition and continued her single-minded commitment to providing assistance where it was needed.

The increased support gained through worldwide media attention as a result of the Nobel Prize helped to put the Missions of Charity on firmer financial ground; but, with the strange twist typical of the Western news industry, Mother Teresa herself quickly became a figure of mass media mythology. Before the Nobel award, she frequently visited crisis locations throughout the world to assess their needs and to set up necessary services. Her arrival at the scene of a tragedy can only be a comfort for those afflicted. While her own motivations and her drive to offer needed care have seen no change, the very presence of Mother Teresa in Ethiopia, for example, or at the scene of the disastrous leak at the chemical plant in Bhopal, India, has provided a focus for the media through which they can reinforce the newsworthiness of these human catastrophes.

While picture opportunities for television, magazines and newspapers may bring attention and relief to a crisis situation, they also divert public awareness from the specific problems of the victims and from the true nature of the work of individuals like Mother Teresa and agencies such as the Missions of Charity. In the atmosphere of such media events as that in which the stooped and wrinkled Catholic nun publicly accepted a much-needed check for Ethiopian refugees from a dramatically garbed and coiffed British rock star under the full glare of television lights, the straightforward photographs by Mary Ellen Mark in this book take on important meaning.

Although Mary Ellen Mark's photographs are now being published half a decade after their making, their passionate and forceful presentation of Mother Teresa's work in Calcutta remains haunting. Not always easy to look at individually, their collective impact is optimistic, for they convey the idea that healing can be attained through human caring. They clearly demonstrate the power of photography to communicate even the most common events of the world in an eloquent and poignant manner.

DAVID FEATHERSTONE is executive associate of The Friends of Photography. He served as editor for The Friends' 1984 publication *Observations, Essays on Documentary Photography (Untitled 35)*; his book *Doris Ulmann: American Portraits* was published in 1985.

*February 27. Early morning, on the way to the railway station, I see a boy asleep on
the dividing island of the highway. I have seen him before in the same spot. I suppose that is where he always sleeps.
He is about ten years old. Sound asleep, he is oblivious to everything.*

CALCUTTA, 1981

People gathered outside the Home for the Dying, 1981

· 14 ·

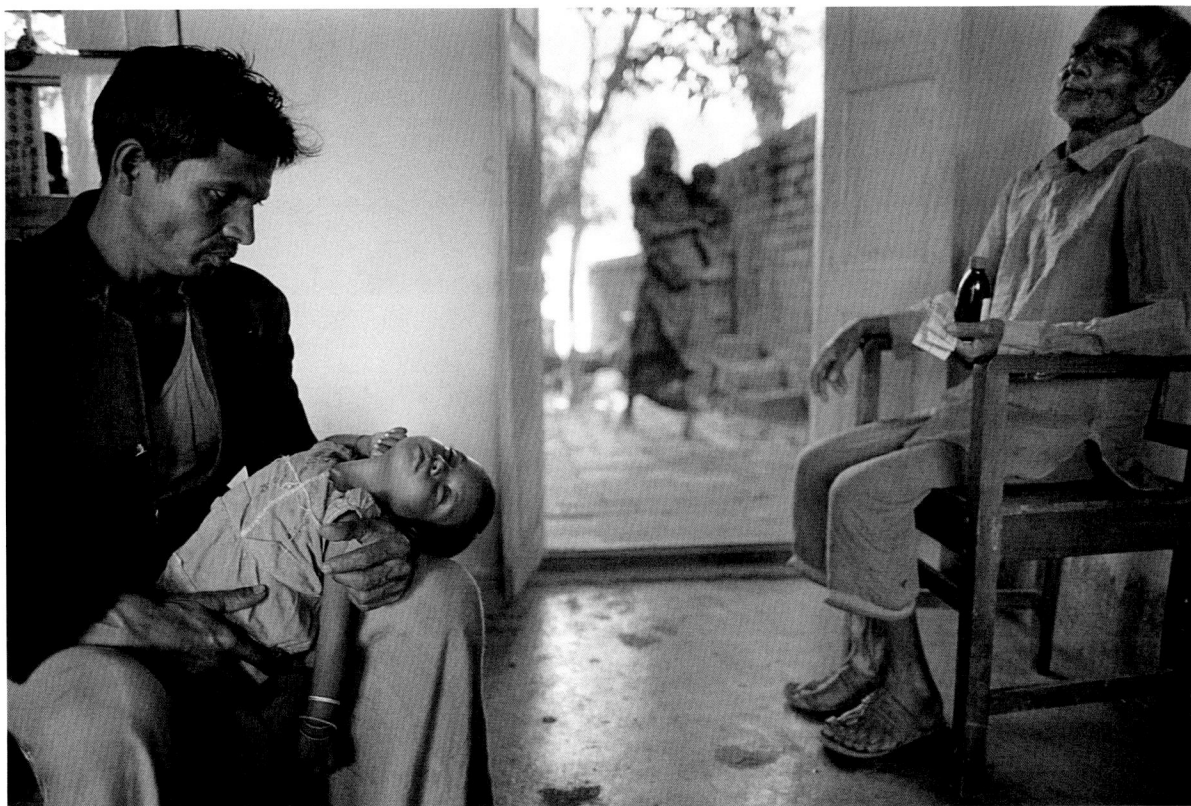

DISPENSARY JUST OUTSIDE OF CALCUTTA, 1981

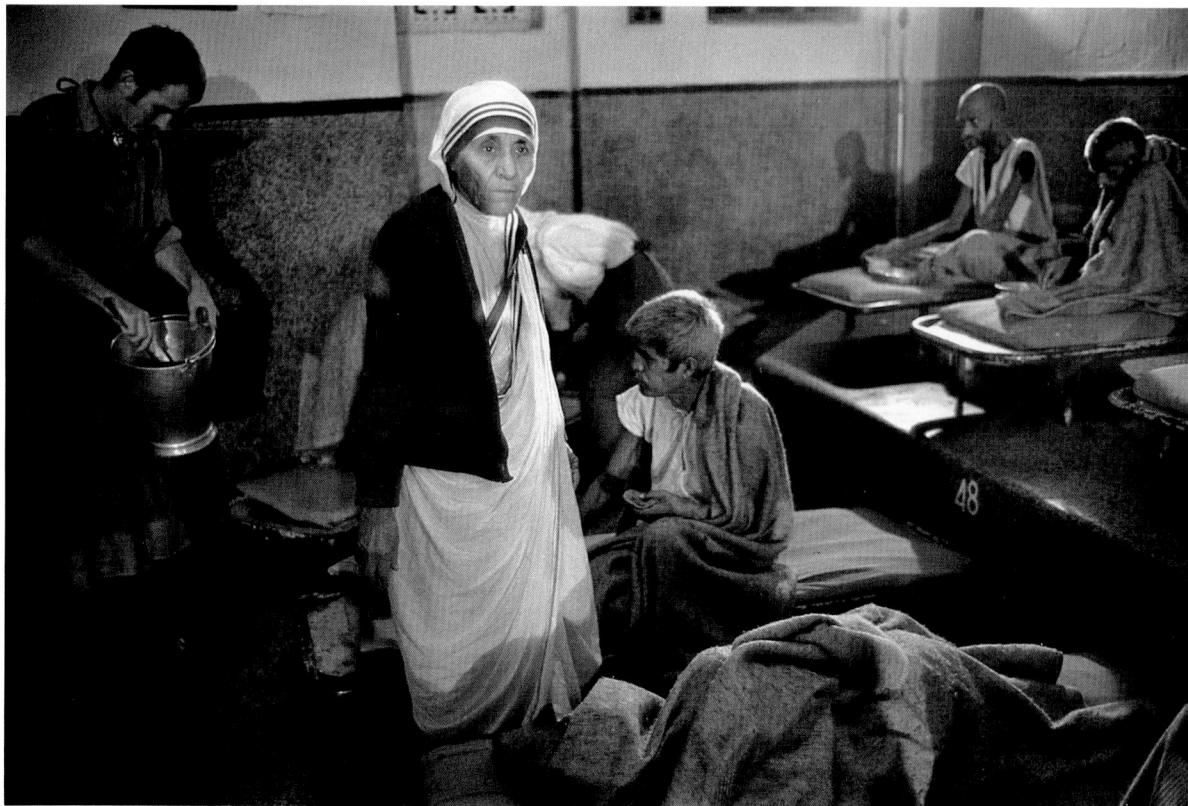

MOTHER TERESA IN NIRMAL HRIDAY, THE HOME FOR THE DYING, 1980

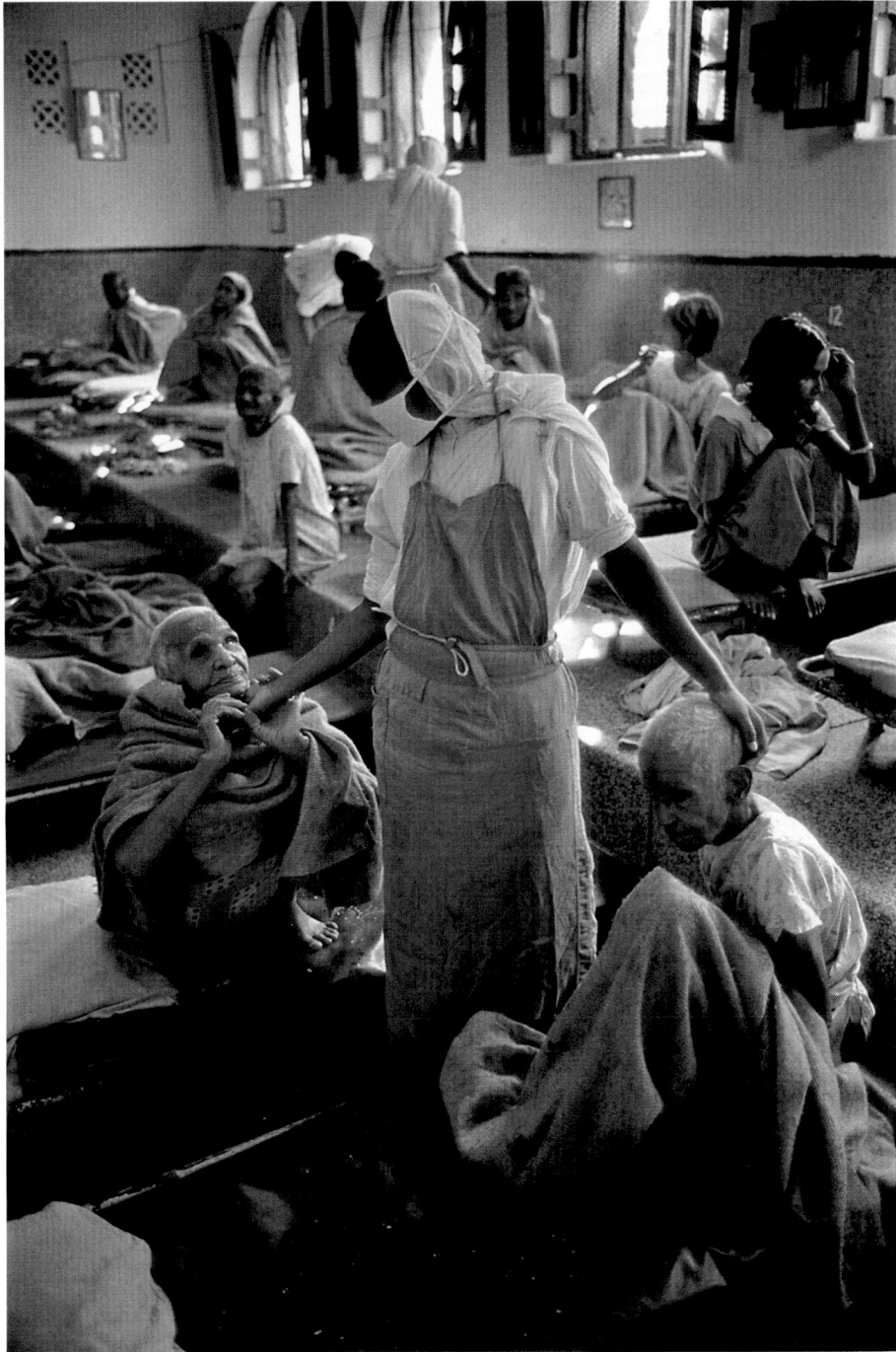

HOME FOR THE DYING, 1980

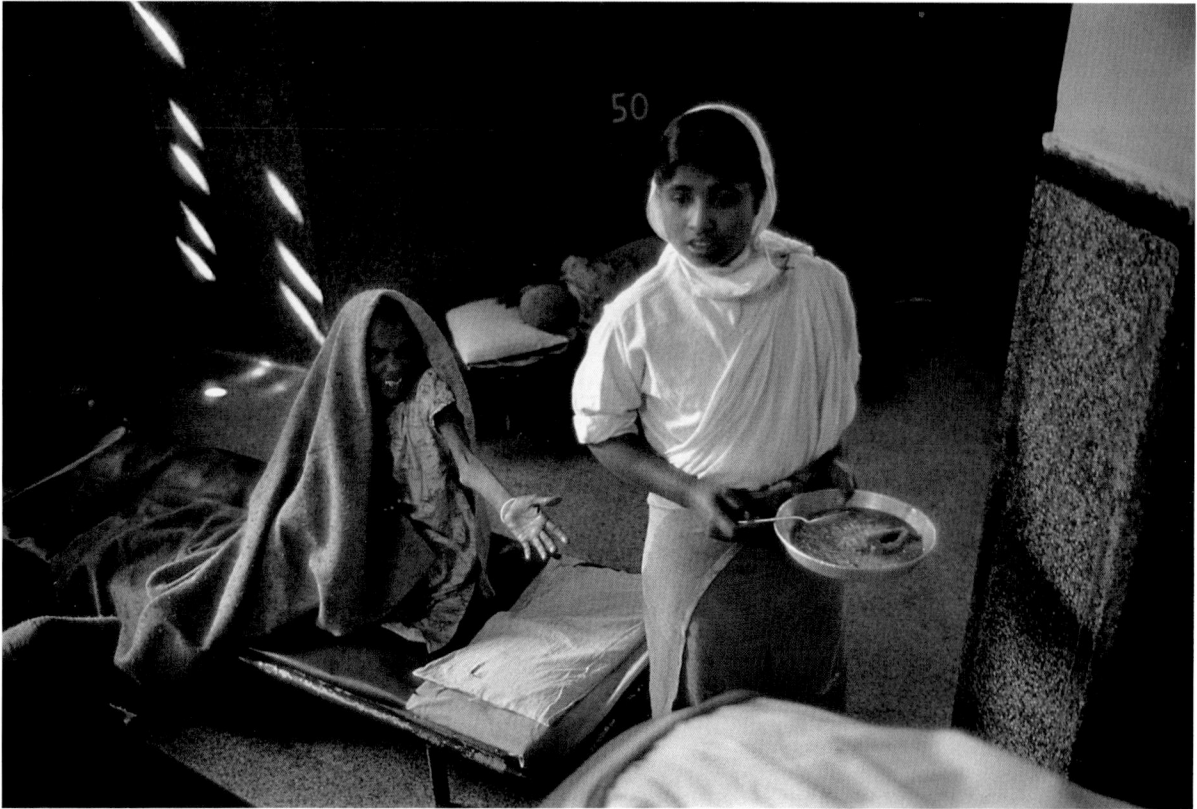

January 24. Some of the women have automatic begging gestures, even though here they have all the food that they could want. They have been begging for so many years that the hand just naturally goes up in a begging gesture.

HOME FOR THE DYING, 1980

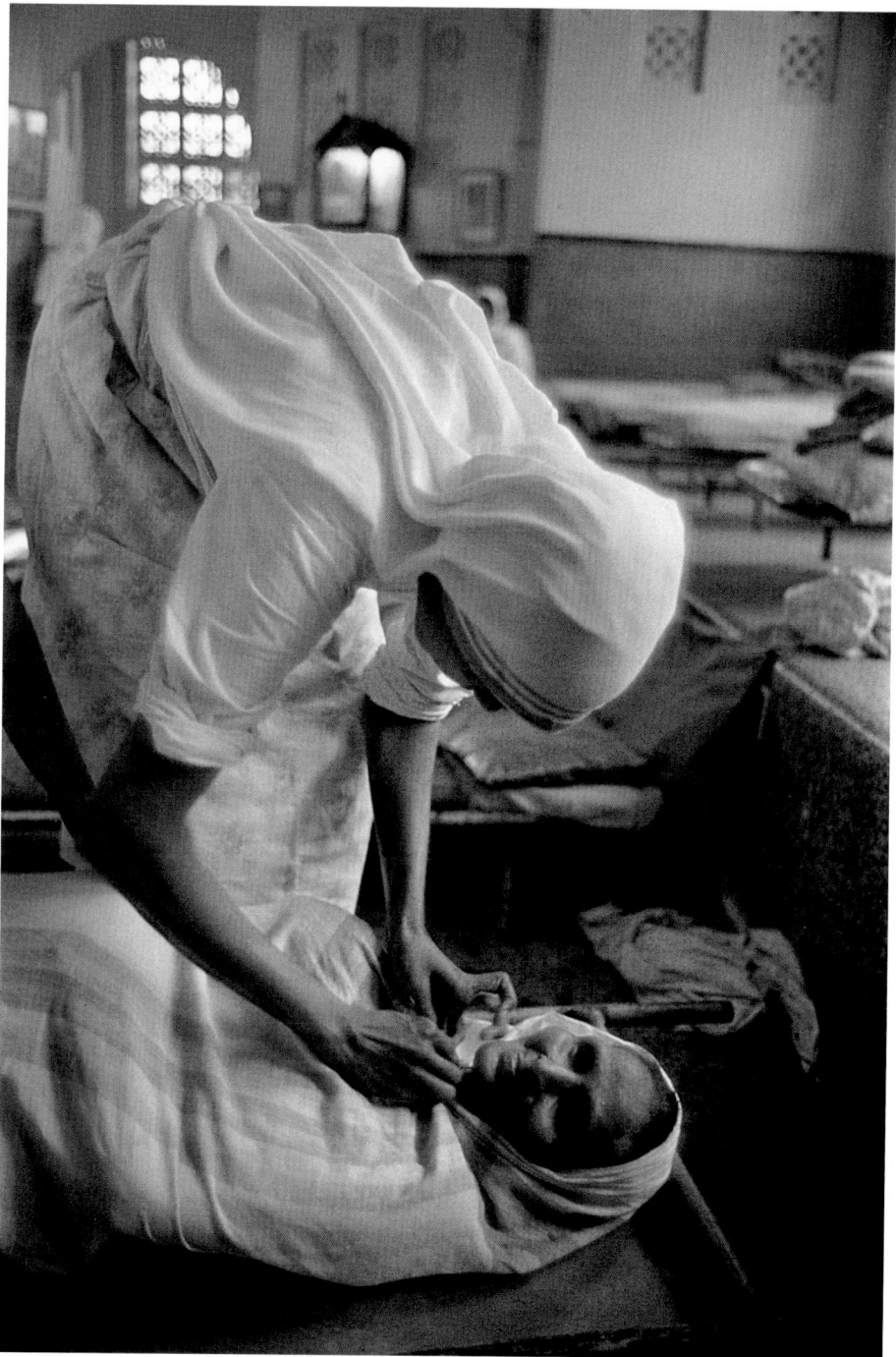

HOME FOR THE DYING, 1980

January 28. Every day the Home for the Dying is cleaned, but once a month it is scrubbed down floor to ceiling.
Work starts at 8:30 a.m., and is not completed until 6:30 p.m. The patients are moved and the furniture aired; the men and women
wait for the nuns to finish the task, and replace them in their beds.

HOME FOR THE DYING, 1980

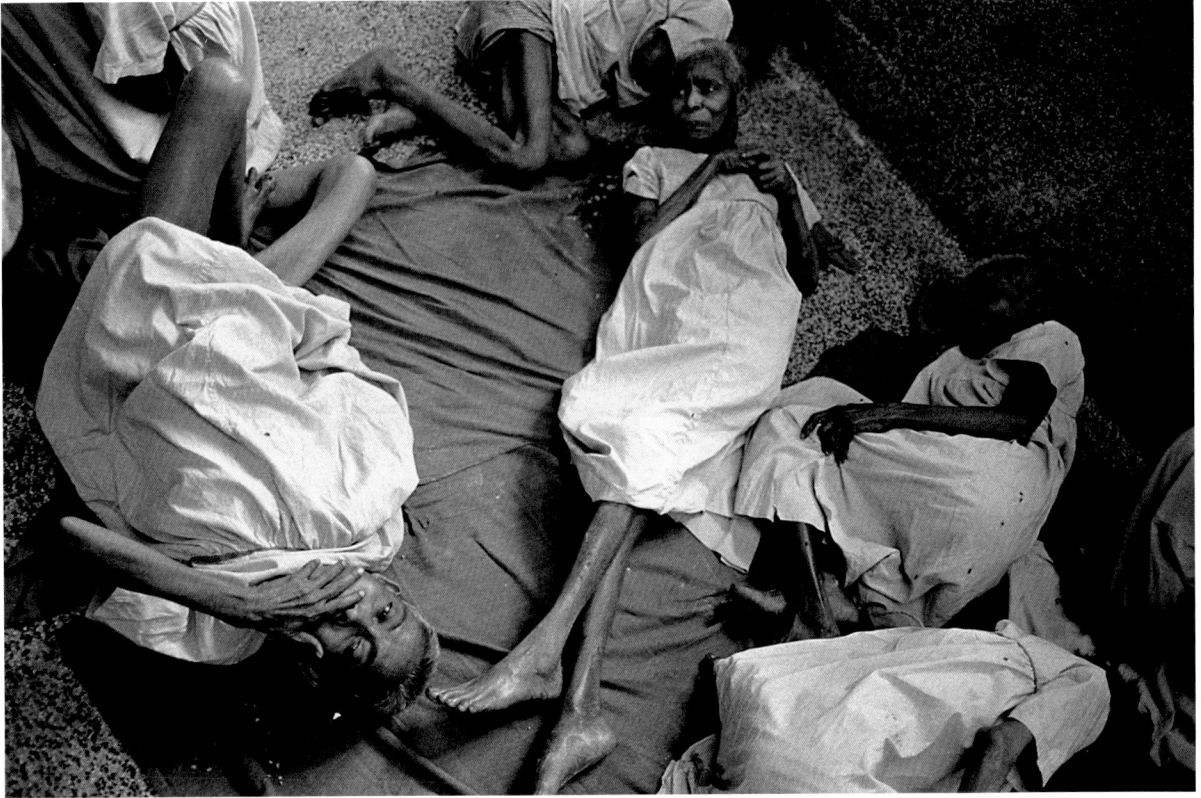

HOME FOR THE DYING, 1980

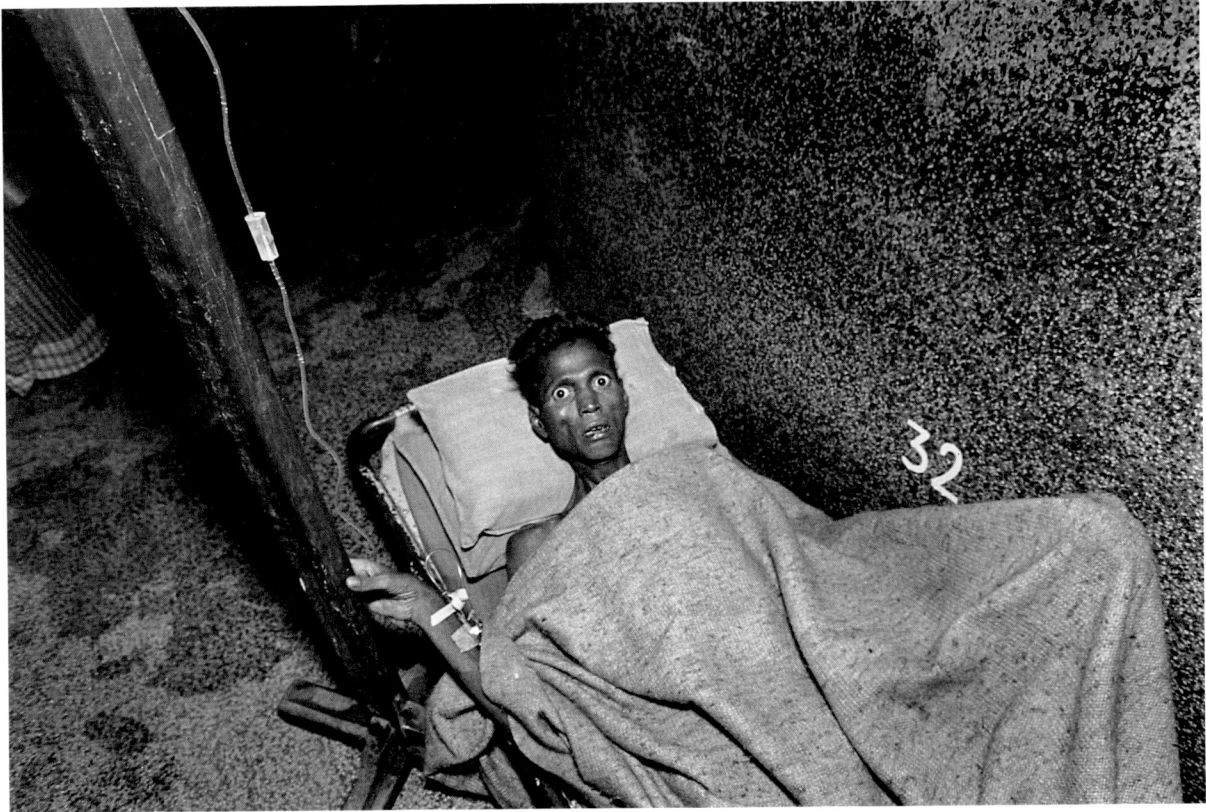

January 27. I watched a man fighting for life, the last stages before death. He tried to stay awake to fight.
He was terrified, restless, trapped in his own body. He definitely knew that he was dying. Sister Luke said,
"The men die much faster than the women, the women take a long time to die."

HOME FOR THE DYING, 1980

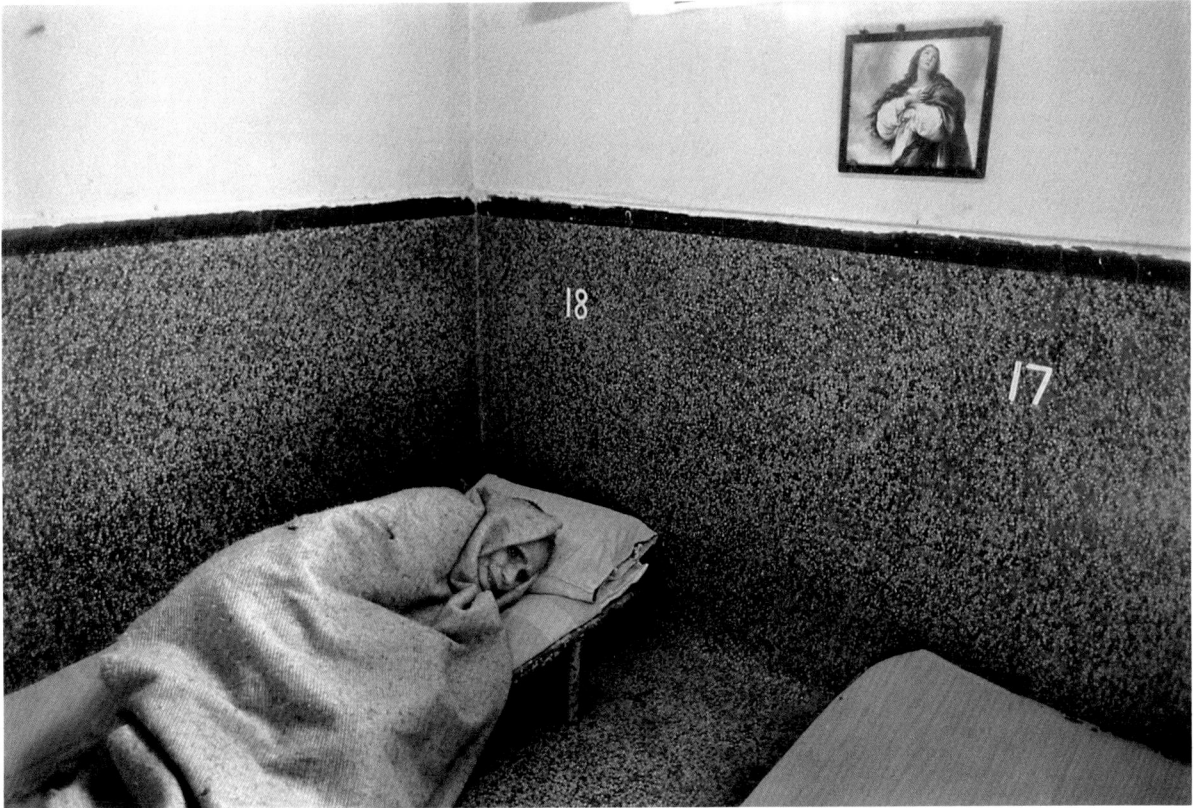

Home for the Dying, 1980

· 23 ·

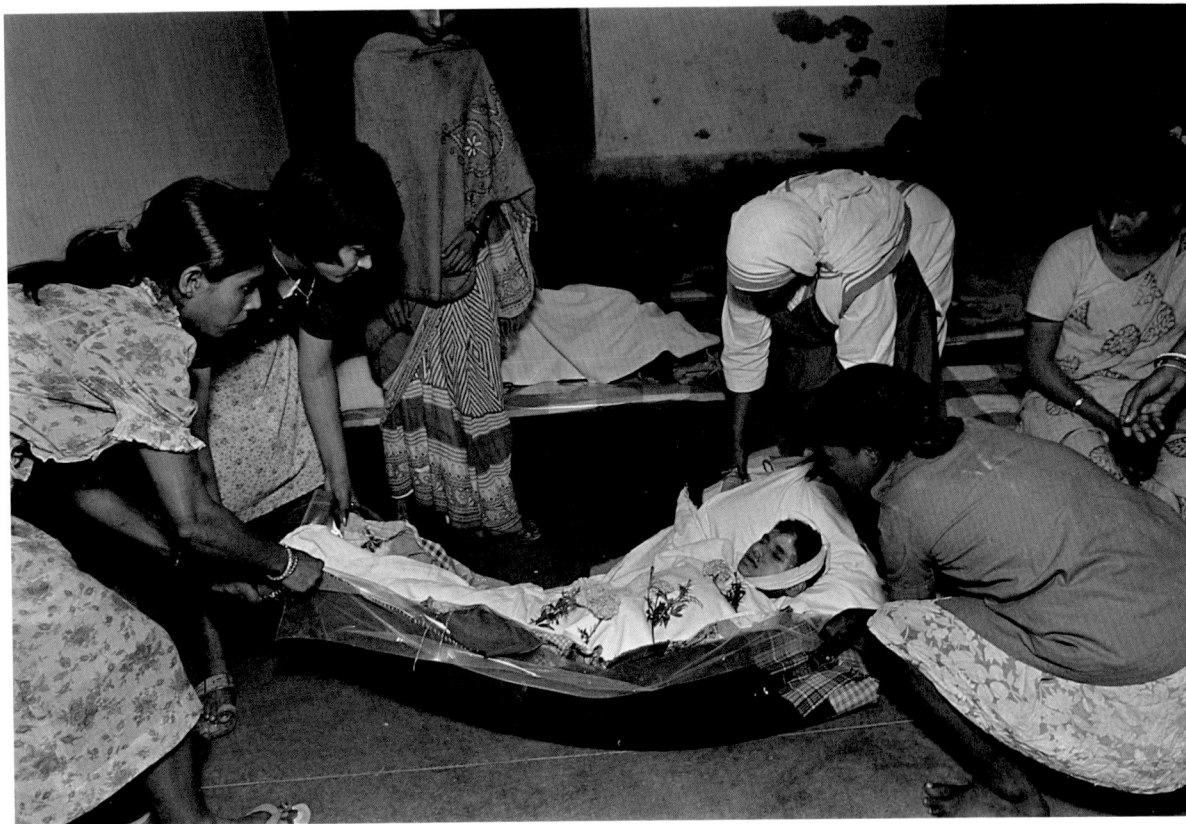

Nurses tending deceased patient at the Kennedy Center for Retarded and Psychotic Women, 1980

MORGUE AT THE HOME FOR THE DYING, 1980

January 24. When a foreigner arrives at the orphanage, all the children cling to you. They are all hoping that you will adopt them. When Shiva first saw me she jumped up and down with glee. One of the sisters told me that she doesn't usually take to strangers. I feel so guilty, I hope she doesn't think that I am here to adopt her.

SHISHU BHAWAN (CHILDREN'S ORPHANAGE), 1980

Blind orphan at Shishu Bhawan, 1980

MOTHER TERESA AT SHISHU BHAWAN, 1980

MOTHER TERESA AT PREM DAN, 1980

Retarded children at Prem Dan, 1981

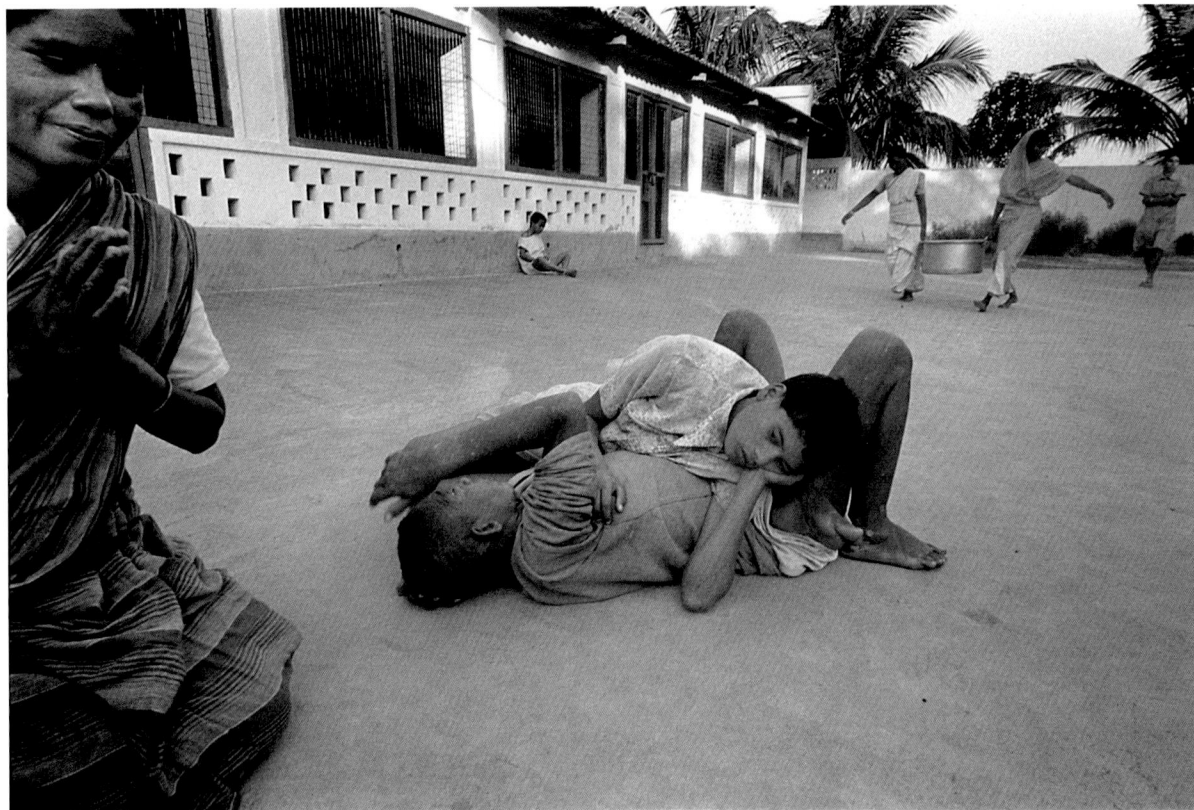

Retarded and psychotic women at Prem Dan, 1980

Two children whose parents are lepers, at Shanti Nagar—Peace Village, 1981

February 18. I walk around the dispensary, the hospital and the village.
There is silence, only the noise of pigs, birds and geese. The people are soaking their wounds.
They bow respectfully; I feel their shame. The sister has told me not to touch them because of infection,
and I am overly aware of this. I wonder, can they tell that I am trying not to touch them?
I ask the sister why there is such silence. Why don't the people cry out? She said,
"This disease is one that isolates; these people have no one to cry out to."

SHANTI NAGAR LEPROSY HOSPITAL, 1981

MOTHER TERESA GIVING COMMUNION IN THE MOTHER HOUSE, 1981

POSTULANTS COMBING AND DRYING THEIR HAIR AT PREM DAN, 1981

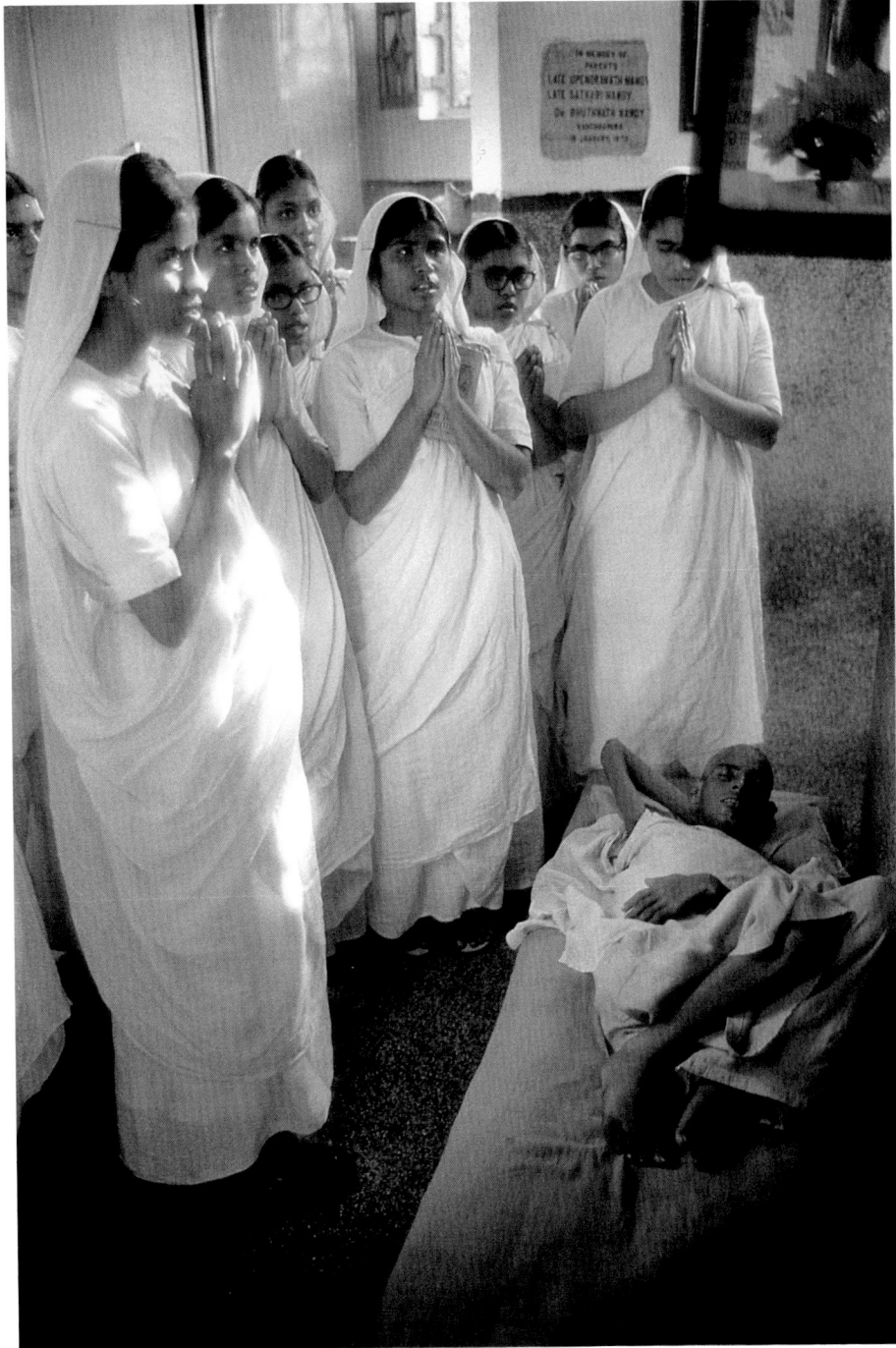

SISTERS PRAYING AT THE HOME FOR THE DYING, 1980

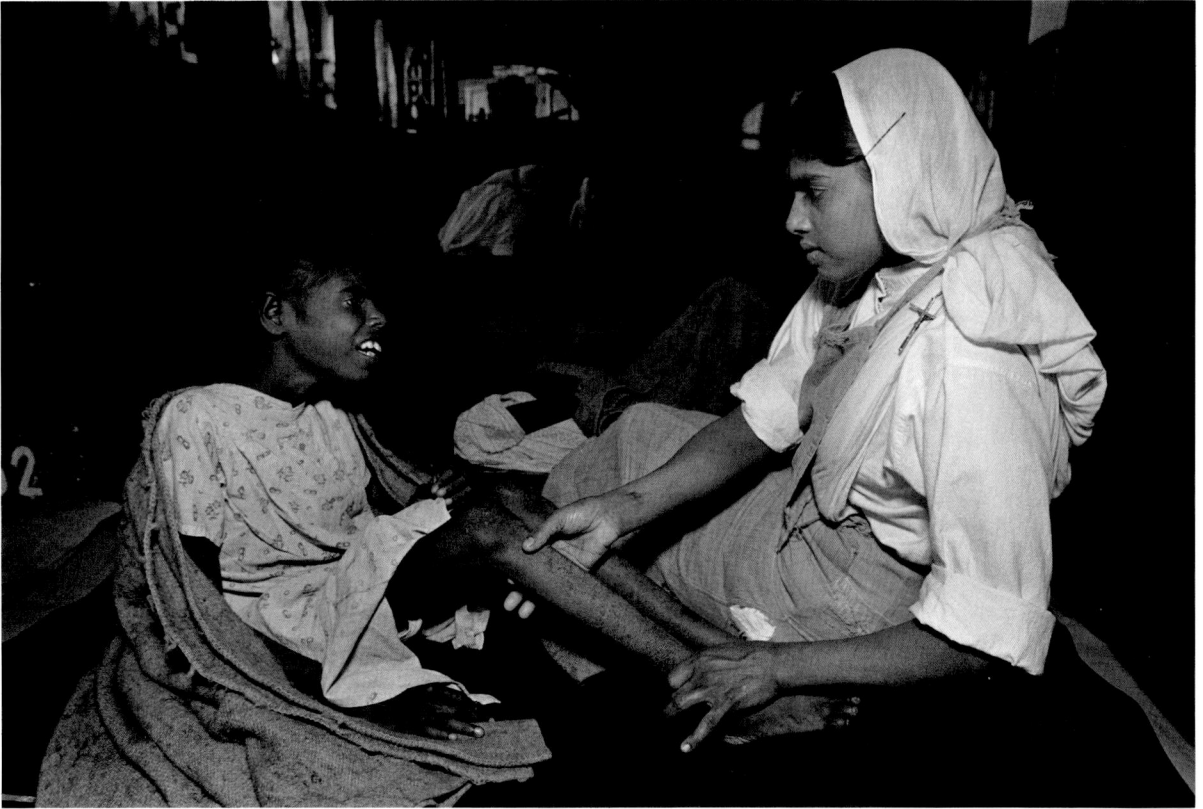

BLIND GIRL AT THE HOME FOR THE DYING, 1980

January 27. Today they brought in a man from the street. They laid him down in the wash area.
He was covered with dirt, and the smell was terrible. The Brothers washed him and soaped him. He was skin and bones.
He looked at me and made a sign with his hand for a cigarette. Sister Luke sent someone out to buy him a pack
of bidis (Indian cigarettes). She was embarrassed, so she asked me to give them to him.
Now all the male patients think that I give out cigarettes.

HOME FOR THE DYING, 1980

· 38 ·

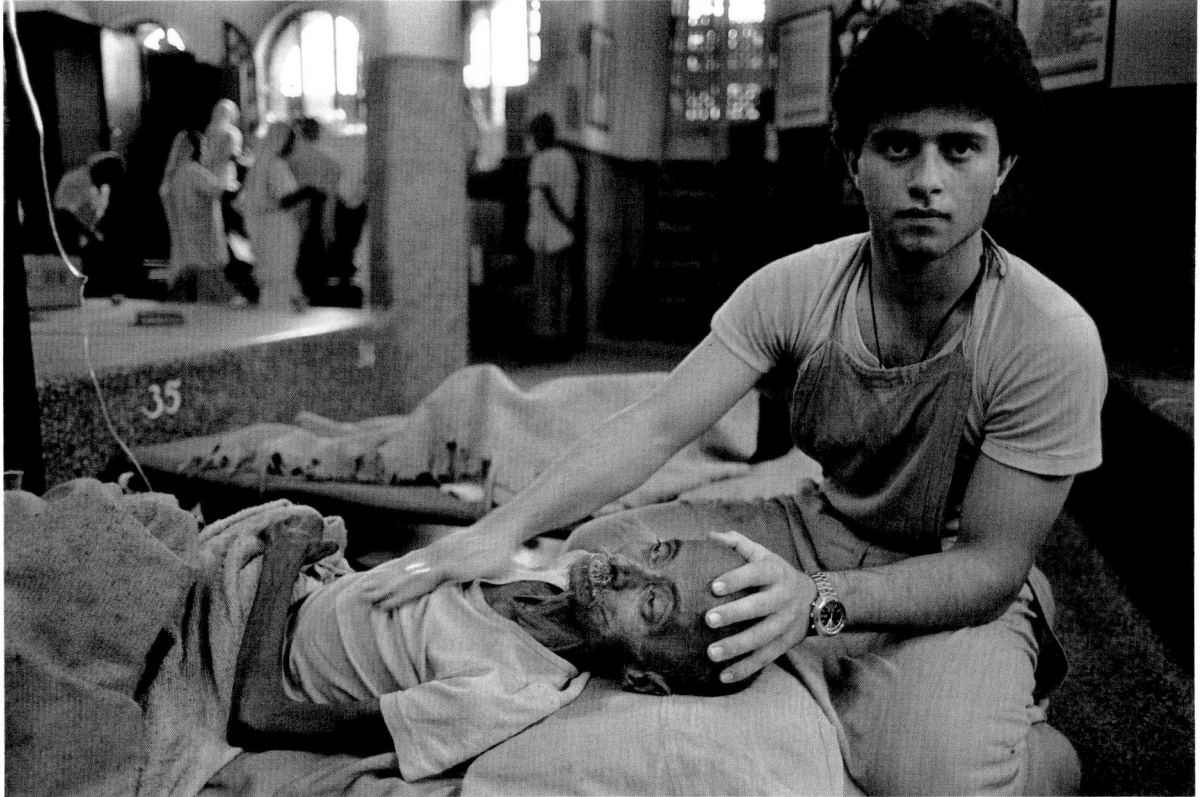

IRANIAN VOLUNTEER IN THE HOME FOR THE DYING, 1981

MOTHER TERESA, MEERUT, 1981

February 1. The cries and suffering of malnutrition, bodies destroyed beyond belief,
limbs that are covered with loose hanging flesh. Women of fifty that look and act ninety; women of forty that look seventy.
Stomach cramps and diarrhea, constant coughing and spitting, the smell of age and decay and excrement all blended together.
The smell is something I cannot forget. It stays in my nostrils even after I return to my hotel room.

HOME FOR THE DYING, 1980

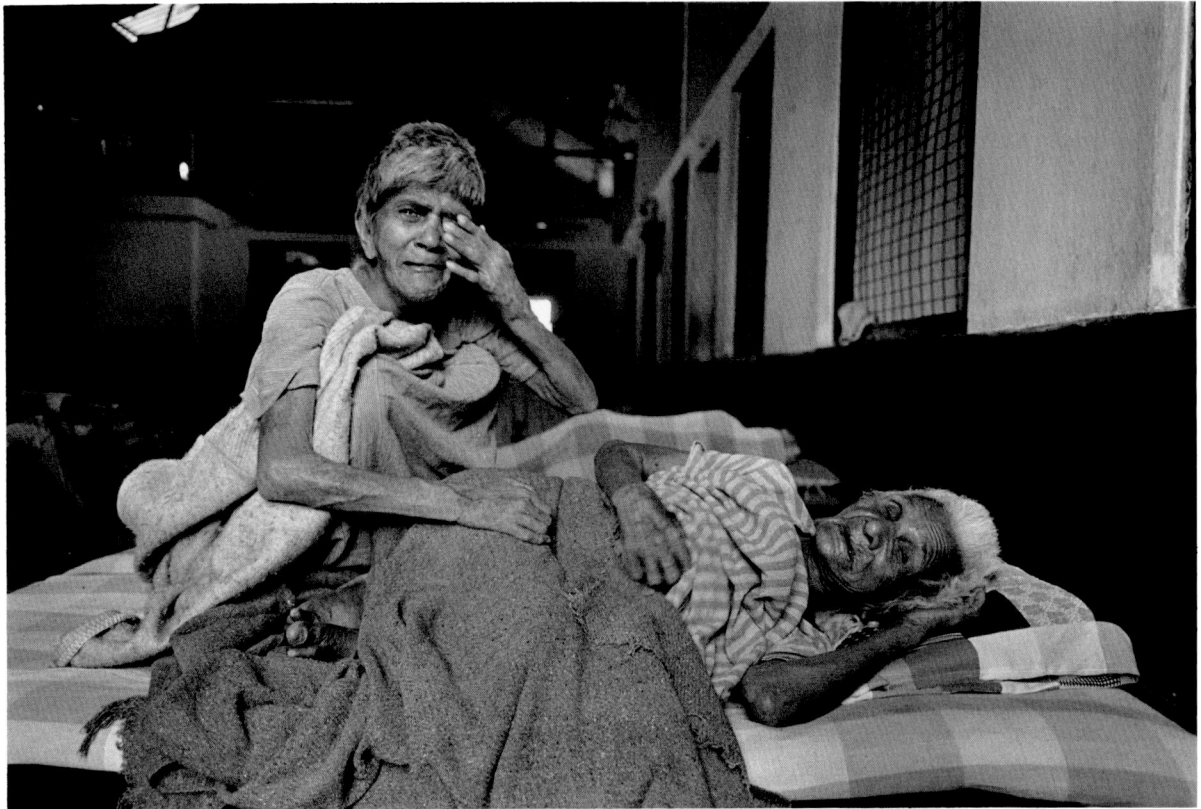

Two blind patients at Prem Dan, 1981

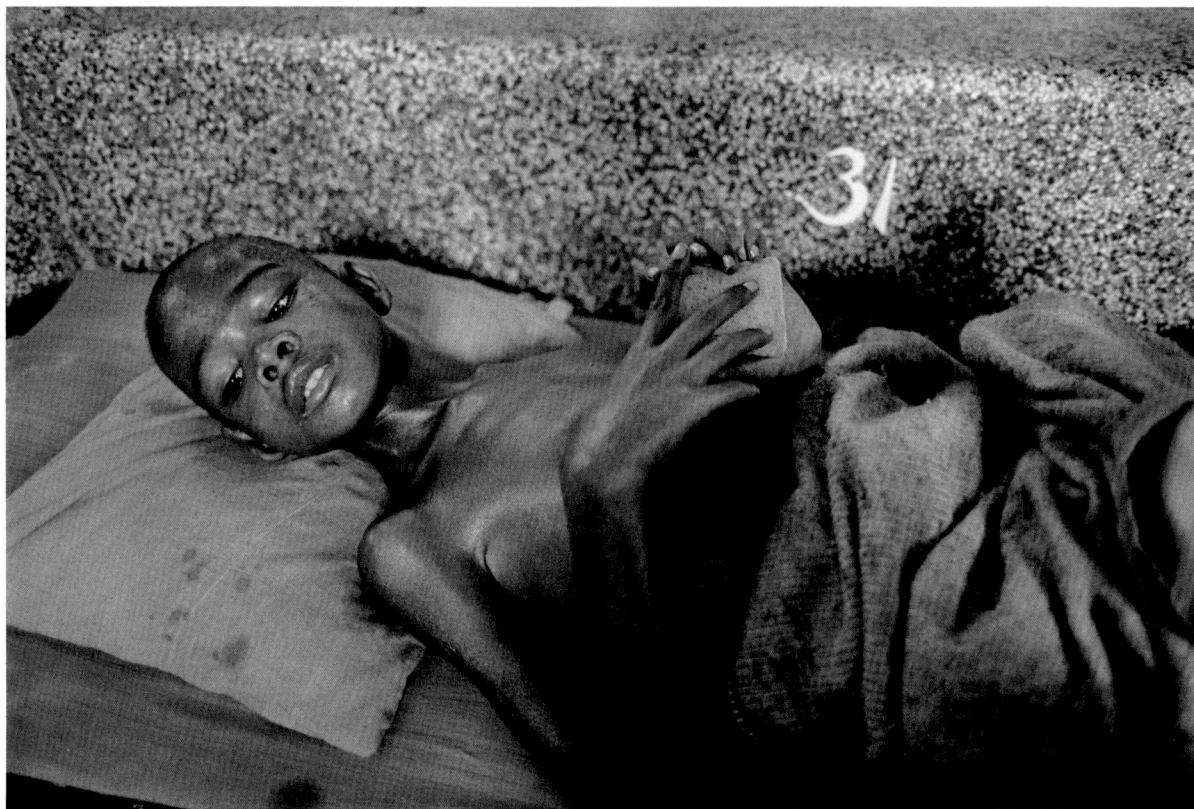

March 7. Today there was a picnic for all the extremely poor children
who live on the streets around Kalighat Temple. Early in the morning, about 400 excited children arrived
at the Home for the Dying to be bathed and dressed in donated clothes before leaving for the picnic in awaiting busses.
I felt terrible for the Home for the Dying patients today, even much more sorrow than I usually feel. The picnic children
were very poor, but they were strong and healthy, real survivors. Today the place was full of laughter and energy.
The poor patients at Kalighat seemed even more defeated and needy. I wish they could get up
from their beds, put on new clothes and go to a picnic.

HOME FOR THE DYING, 1981

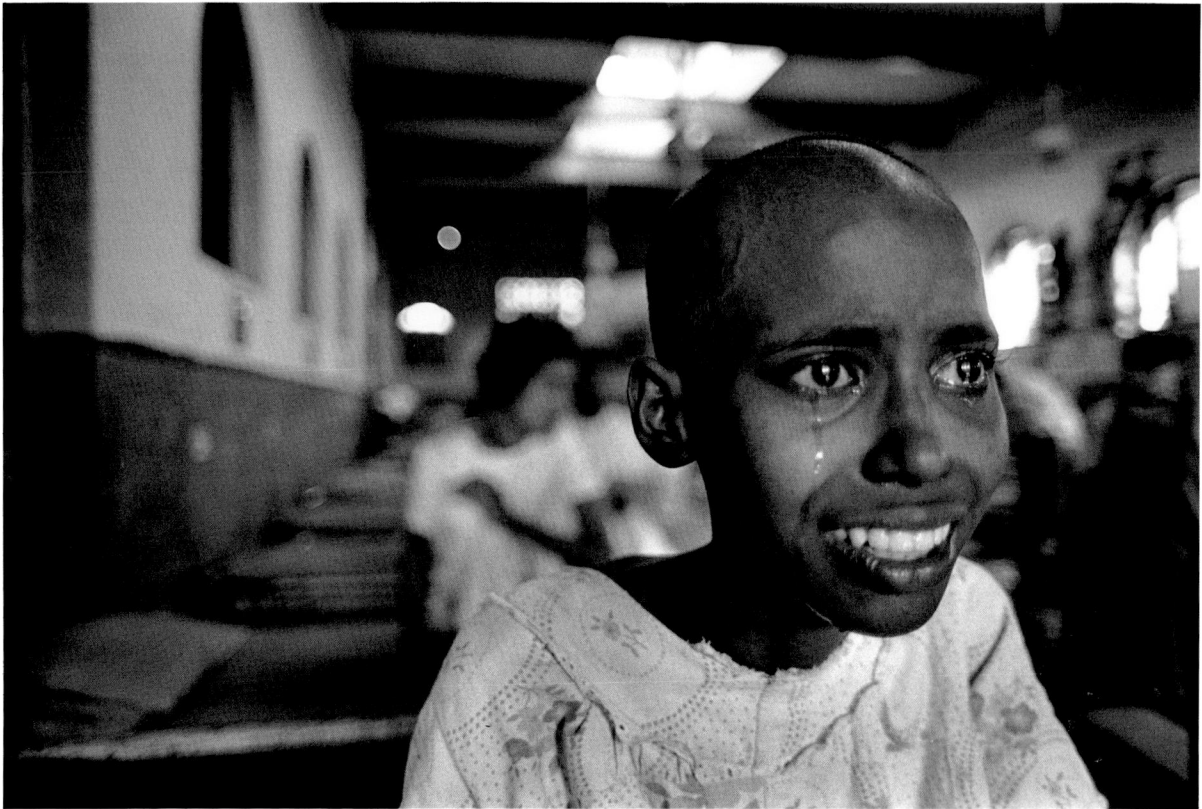

February 27. The beautiful young girl with the big eyes and long lashes is crying. She wants to leave.
She is so thin and weak that she will surely die if she goes. She keeps going outside and asking for a sari,
and the sisters have to carry her back. Her eyes are huge and wild. She won't take her medicine, so Sister Luke threatens
to put a tube down her throat. She finally takes her medicine, but all day long she continues to walk outside,
ask for a sari and cry. I found out that her name is Goudi.

HOME FOR THE DYING, 1981

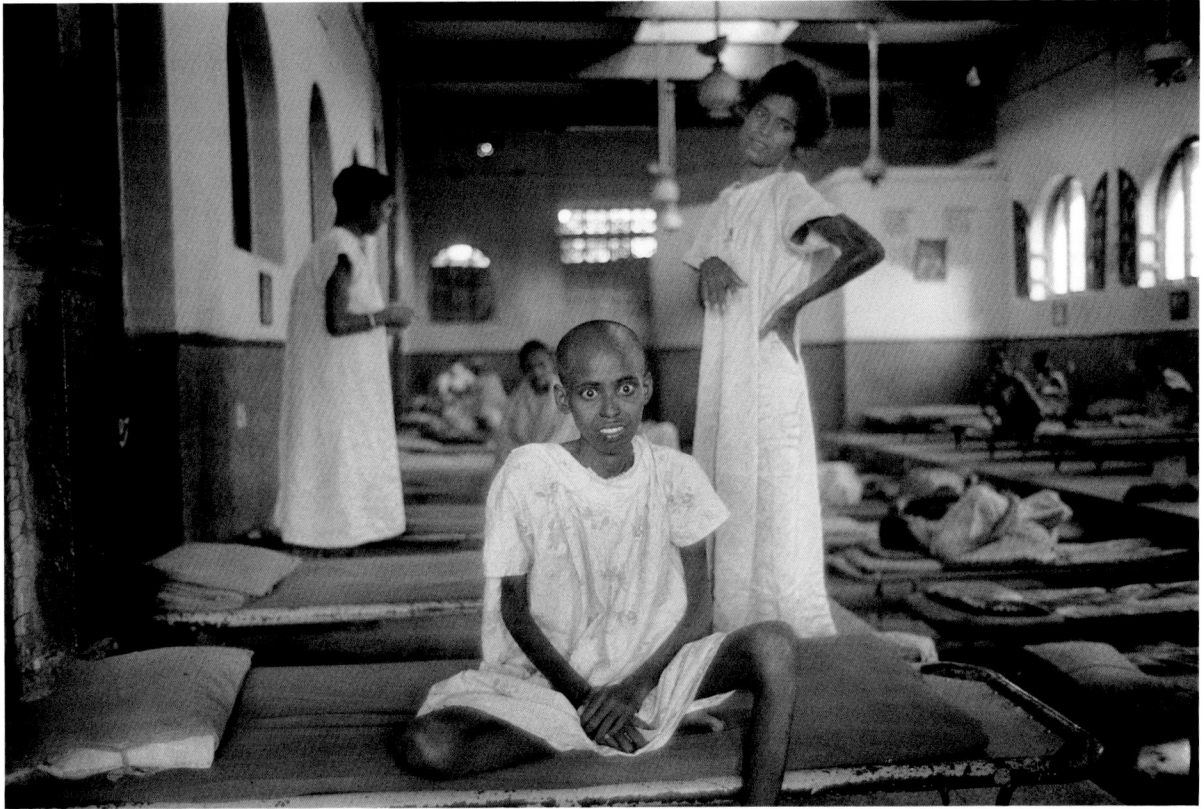

GOUDI AT THE HOME FOR THE DYING, 1981

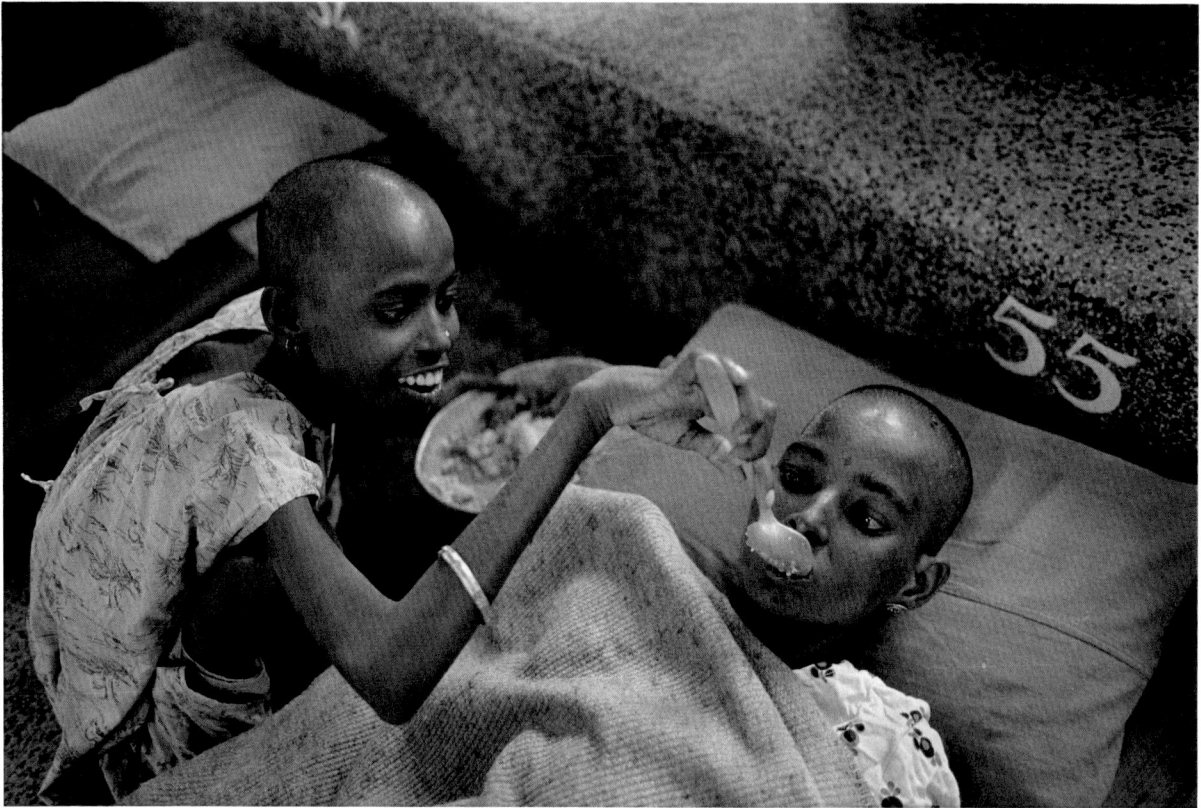

March 3. Today a beautiful girl was brought in that looked just like Goudi, but a bit older and even thinner. Goudi noticed the resemblance, and immediately came up to her, but the girl turned away. Later, when food was being served, she took a plate and fed her. Goudi really confuses me. A few days ago she was hysterical wanting to leave. Today she is all smiles, and is even ordering me around, asking me to squeeze orange juice for her new friend.

HOME FOR THE DYING, 1981

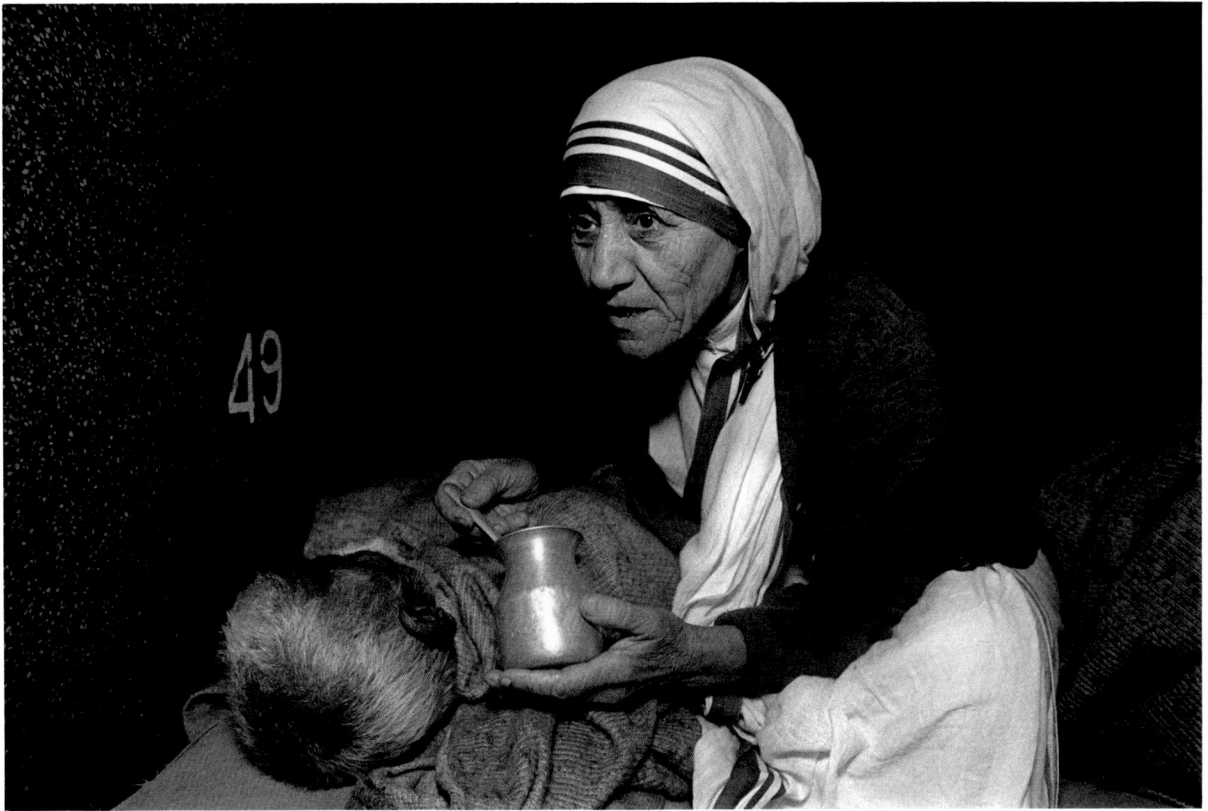

MOTHER TERESA AT THE HOME FOR THE DYING, CALCUTTA, 1980

THE FRIENDS OF PHOTOGRAPHY,
founded in 1967, is a not-for-profit membership organization with headquarters in Carmel, California. The programs of The Friends in publications, grants and awards to photographers, exhibitions, workshops and lectures are guided by a commitment to photography as a fine art, and to the discussion of photographic ideas through critical inquiry. The publications of The Friends, the primary benefit received by members of the organization, emphasize contemporary photography yet are also concerned with the criticism and history of the medium. They include a monthly newsletter, the journal *Untitled* and major photographic monographs. Membership is open to everyone. To receive an informational membership brochure, write to the Membership Coordinator, The Friends of Photography, Post Office Box 500, Carmel, California 93921.